Interface
California Corporation
Eureka

Fine California Views
the photographs of A.W. Ericson

by PETER E. PALMQUIST

To

A. W. Ericson

He documented his adopted land
with both pride and foresight.

The author wishes to thank the many persons who have aided him in the preparation of this monograph. Although the limitations of space make it impossible to acknowledge each of you by name, your interest and willing help have provided support in my investigations, and answers to my many questions. There are a few individuals who, through their active participation, deserve individual mention. Among these, Genelle and Bob Dolezal have provided valuable insight and editorial assistance when it was needed, and facilitated the design and production of the book. The staff of Interface California Corporation also deserves special recognition. Mrs. Percy J. Bryan, Dr. Robert V. Bryan, and Mrs. Ivan Krestensen are to be thanked for their active interest and material aid, both with facts and the sharing of family records.

Many individuals have aided in preparation of the manuscript. Among these, the author thanks Mrs. Frances Purser, Mr. Erich Schimps, Mr. Andrew Genzoli, Mr. Lynwood Carranco, Mr. Micheal Hurd, Ms. Joan Naves, Mr. J. W. (Bill) Lundberg and Mr. James G. Lundberg for their hard work in checking facts and reviewing the written text.

Finally, I especially wish to thank Sally, my wife, for her continued support and interest.

Table of Contents

Augustus William Ericson
1848-1927

Introduction

One might wonder that an entire book is devoted to a previously obscure and little-known photographer. Why not a re-examination of established figures such as Edward Curtis, Eadweard Muybridge, or William H. Jackson? Augustus William Ericson has remained relatively unknown and without the recognition he richly deserves despite widespread display of many of his photographic images, which have appeared repeatedly throughout the years without proper credit. A glance through the portfolio portion of this book will quickly reveal his unique contribution to the documentary art. This effort, then, is an attempt to share the personal excitement and enthusiasm of the author with regard to Ericson's photographs.

National repositories such as the *Smithsonian* and the *Library of Congress*, as well as many regional institutions, have long held Ericson images. The State of California and the *Oakland Museum*, among others, have used A. W. Ericson's photographs as an integral part of their thematic displays dealing with anthropological materials. His photographs of northern California Indians and early-day redwood logging rate among the best in existence. Textbooks have widely reproduced illustrations of his images in these areas. Thus, while portions of Ericson's work have obtained limited recognition, the bulk of his images and his personal life have remained obscure.

In 1964, A. W. Ericson's works returned to public access when his youngest daughter, Mrs. Percy J. (Ella) Bryan, donated 128 8- X 10-inch glass plates to the library of Humboldt State University in Arcata, California. This assemblage, together with subsequent donations of more than 360 additional negatives, formed the basis for a permanent Ericson collection. Today Humboldt State University is the largest single holder of Ericson photography. Credit for recognition of the historical significance of this material may be placed with Mrs. Frances Purser, librarian for the university from 1960 to 1972.

The author's first contact with the Ericson images took place when he was called upon by Mrs. Purser to reproduce copy negatives and file prints from the original Ericson glass plates and prints. As the wide diversity of the collection became apparent, it stimulated a growing enthusiasm and respect. He soon found himself seeking additional information on Ericson that has lead to the publication of this monograph.

A. W. Ericson did not come to America as a photographer. He wished, as did so many pilgrims, to participate in the rich opportunities that were an important part of the "American Dream." In Ericson's day, this dream was one not only of promised wealth and success, but also of personal fulfillment. Ericson found that the United States, in 1866, was not a country paved with gold. The Civil War had just ended. Barely 18 years of age, he had neither money nor adequate education, and did not speak English. An apprentice printer in Sweden, he became in turn, a laborer in Chicago, woodsman in Michigan, and millhand, bookkeeper, clerk, telegrapher and shopkeeper in California. It was during this last period, sometime after 1880, that A. W. Ericson turned his attention to photography in the coastal community of Arcata.

Although it is difficult to identify the precise moment when photography became important to him, Ericson's inquisitive nature and friendship with local studio operators surely served to stimulate and quicken his interest. As yet, no evidence suggests that Ericson became involved in photography during the wet plate era. It may well have been the announcement of the gelatin dry plate process that prompted him to become an amateur practitioner of photography. The skill quickly became a natural extension of his need to express himself.

Ericson's images recall his personal satisfaction at the harnessing of the redwood wilderness into a productive union of settlers and opportunists. He clearly recognized the importance of photography as a permanent document of progress. Starting in the burgeoning 1880's, and for the nearly 40 years which followed, he photographed a coastal region extending from the Oregon border on the north, to Monterey, California on the south. Humboldt County, located in the northern extremity of this area was both his home and favorite subject.

During Ericson's active period of photography, opportunities in logging, shipbuilding, mining, and farming drew settlers to Humboldt County in increasing numbers. Towns grew rapidly, and the need for housing and business services expanded to booming proportions. Ericson sought to record each detail. He photographed the felling and milling of giant redwoods, coastal shipping, construction of new homes and businesses, introduction of steam power, groups of school children, railroads, holiday excursions, agriculture, and the bustle of everyday life. His pictures of the white deerskin dance and other Indian rituals are ranked among the best examples of such photographs in the nation. In later years, he recorded the advent of electricity, arrival of the first motorcar, and a multitude of changes that resulted from the growth of the Twentieth Century.

Although his portraits were popular, Ericson's best work was exhibited in his scenic views. Characteristically, these views were a contact-printed 8- X 10-inch glass plate image on an 11- X 14-inch mount, with typeset caption. At least 35 years of age when he started photography, he used his camera until two years before his death in 1927. His most significant work occurred from the late 1880's until the advent of World War I.

Ericson took his photography seriously. He carried his Eastman 8 X 10 field camera great distances by horse and buggy, often camping until he obtained the "view" he was after. He was a careful workman and insisted that every aspect of development, printing and mounting be precisely accomplished. Ericson's images have a straight-forward significance; however, his style remains essentially a documentary record rather than manipulation for artistic content. His views are solid without pretension. Most include people, as if he wished to show an essential link of man with his environment as well as to provide scale.

In the decades which followed A. W. Ericson's death in 1927, his reputation grew. Today, he is remembered by local residents of Arcata as "the man who took those old pictures." Such a distinction becomes notable only if one considers that, while nearly 130 professional photographers practiced in the Humboldt County area between 1850 and 1930, only Ericson is uniquely remembered. A few octogenarians remember Ericson vividly for his gentleman-dandy dress and congenial social manner.

America has had many photographers; only a handful have had the unique sense of destiny that caused them to diligently devote a large portion of their lives to the process of completing a meaningful visual document. Ericson's photographs provide one such insight into history, through their record of the economic and social growth of nineteenth century California frontier into twentieth century modernity. For this reason, his photographs succeed, in the same manner that photographs taken by the pioneer wet plate photographers during the geologic and mapping expeditions of the 1860's and 1870's were successful. They communicate the assets and beauty of a land coming of age.

A. W. Ericson: A Life Chronology

1848-1866: Orebro, Sweden

Born on April 26, 1848 in the important provincial capital of Orebro, Sweden, Augustus William Ericson is believed to be the third child of six born to Eric and Elsa Ericson. The young boy's grandparents had been farmers and tilled the low-lying soil near Lake Hjalmar, about 100 miles west of Stockholm. His father, however, divided his time between the family farm and a job as a printer at the Lindska Printing Works in Orebro.

Little is known of A. W. Ericson's childhood. Orebro was, in 1848, the chief town of a province of that name. Many of its buildings dated from the 14th and 15th centuries. On a small island in the Svarta River stood an impressive 13th century castle. The town, because of its size and importance, was a center for commerce and a market for local farm produce. Iron, zinc and copper mines dotted the surrounding countryside.

Despite his prosperous surroundings, A. W. Ericson received only a scant elementary education. At age 11, he followed his older brother into the printing trade and was apprenticed. He worked at the printing trade until 1866, when he left Orebro and Sweden to come to the United States of America.

The Ericson family home in Orebro, Sweden

1866-1868: Chicago and Michigan

A. W. Ericson's decision to leave Sweden was unpopular with his parents, and little evidence exists today to explain his sudden departure. Possible explanations for his move include the prospect of adventure with a close friend, Charles Johnson. Later correspondance suggests that Johnson and Ericson may have traveled to the United States together, with Johnson returning to Sweden after a few years. Another likely possibility is that he traveled west at the invitation of a family friend already in the United States. This latter explanation seems the most likely, for A. W. Ericson spent little time in New York, as was common for new arrivals to the United States. Instead, he traveled almost immediately to Chicago, where he found employment for a year and one-half. Unable to speak English, he worked as a laborer transforming a cemetery into present-day Lincoln Park. During this time, he made several friends among residents of Chicago's Swedish population, and later corresponded with them for many years.

Tiring of the laborer's life in Chicago, and perhaps drawn by the prospect of higher wages, A. W. Ericson traveled northeast from Chicago in 1868. Near Whitehall, Michigan, he worked for a time in a lumbering camp. After a short stay, he left the woods of northern Michigan and traveled by rail to San Francisco.

1869-1876: Trinidad, California

Upon arrival in the bustling port city of San Francisco, Ericson may have been approached for employment by scouts of either the *Trinidad Mill Company* or *Smith and Dougherty Mill Company.* Without doubt, he had heard stories of northern California, a land where trees reached to the clouds with trunks so large that they could not be encircled by 12 men. After a short stay in San Francisco, he traveled 240 miles north by steamer along the rugged California coast, and disembarked at the lumbering town of Trinidad.

Trinidad was located about 70 miles south of the Oregon border, and had been an important seaport during the Trinity River gold rush of 1850-1852. Swarms of miners laden with supplies had swelled the town to nearly 3000 persons for a few years, but by Ericson's arrival the population numbered only about 200. Two large sawmills with their oxen-driven railways, boarding houses and company stores nestled behind a rocky headland with nearly 60 houses left abandoned by the departing miners. To the east, huge forests of redwood and fir provided timber for the town's economy.

Following his arrival, A. W. Ericson was hired as a laborer, building and maintaining the logging rails. Over these rails, teams of oxen or mules would pull tramcars laden with logs. Ericson quickly improved his command of the English language, teaching himself to read and write. He was later promoted to driver on the railway.

In mid-1871, A. W. Ericson returned briefly to his home in Orebro, Sweden. Little is known about the trip, but it seems to have marked a turning point in his life. Prior to his visit to Sweden, Ericson had kept close ties with his family in Orebro. Upon his return to Trinidad, he appears to have made a commitment to his adopted land and began to make friendships and participate in its society.

While en route from Sweden to Trinidad, Ericson purchased a small dairy, and entered the date 22nd August, 1871 on its flyleaf. This journal, extending from August 1871 to September 1872, illustrates better than any other existant document Ericson's life in Trinidad:

> Thursday, September 21, 1871:
> ". . .On board Schooner *Lola* bound for Trinidad. . ."
> Friday, September 29:
> "Been eadging [sic] the whole day. To night [sic] my hands is very

sore through the handling of the heavy timber and railroad ties."

Tuesday, October 10:

". . .Send [sic] off a letter to Charlie Smith, Arcata. Many Indians have been around the mill today."

Sunday, October 29:

"Been walking around down the warf [sic] and up town. The boss came around little after noon and asked me to take the old job back on the logging train, which I did."

Sunday, November 5:

"In the morning was down to the warf [sic]. *Lola* left at 10 o'clock, and the brig *Crimea* arrived little after. In the afternoon was up and had a look at the lighthouse and its machinery. The weather been beautiful."

Wednesday, November 8:

"Been working on the train the whole day and made four trips. I got a new man this morning instead of John Darches. 9 o'clock and Allen had a fight with the China cook in the woods about lunch. . ."

Saturday, November 11:

"Been working the whole day. In the morning we made two trips with logs and afternoon two trips with wood. At night been to the G. T. [Good Templars] Lodge. The morning was rainy but afternoon fine."

Monday, November 20:

"Been working on the train the whole day and made two trips. At noon [Jack] got his finger hurt on the winch and in the forenoon Charley Johnson, a Swede, got run over by the log car at the new mill, but not killed."

Sunday, December 10:

"This day have past [sic] away very fast. Little after dinner I had a walk up in the woods and around the school house. Later been picking mussels. The weather been beautiful and warm all day."

Wednesday, December 27:

"Been working all day on the train and made five trips. The weather been rainy all day. Most of the boys have headache today after the Christmas drinking."

Thursday, January 4, 1872:

". . .The weather been beautiful all day. Tonight I have a narrow escape from a falling redwood tree."

Wednesday, January 10:

"Have not been working in case of hard wind this morning. Several trees blew down across the train breaking it down badly. This morning I had a narrow escape from two trees."

Friday, February 9:

"Been working all day about the pond raising sinkers and breaking out logs. The weather been rainy."

Wednesday, March 13:

"Been working the whole day on the train and made God knows how many trips about 10 or 12. At night went up to the P.O. [Post Office] but did not get anything. The weather beautiful."

Wednesday, April 3:

". . .This morning Lorance Aimes took poison and afternoon died. 7 o'clock was up to a meeting for the funeral. At night send off a letter to friend Chs. Johnson."

Trinidad, California in the early days

The *Trinidad Mill Company* Store

Friday, May 31:

"...The weather been beautiful. At night heard a lecture at the G.T. [Good Templars] Hall on "Women" by Miss Anne Morrison."

Sunday, June 23:

"Early this morning Chs. Thompson and myself went out picking blackberries. Later went up town and at 2 o'clock attended the Sunday school. At night attended the G.T. [Good Templars] meeting. Had four visitors from Arcata."

By the time A. W. Ericson's diary ended on September 14, 1872, his writing had progressed from early entries in Swedish, through a barely legible, poorly-spelled scrawl in English, into a much neater, well-defined hand. He avidly devoured all available journals and newspapers to improve his command of English. His fellow workers increasingly came to Ericson, asking him to compose letters to friends and handle business transactions. He held, in turn, both the position of finance secretary and recording secretary for his lodge, the Independent Order of Good Templars, No. 400.

As his education improved, Ericson was promoted by the *Trinidad Mill Company* from his job in the woods crew to the position of bookkeeper. During this period, he learned to operate the telegraph, and was exposed to shop keeping at the company store. In 1876, a recession slowed lumber sales and many men were layed off their jobs. A. W. Ericson continued to work at the Trinidad mill until the fall of 1876, when he moved 15 miles south to the community of Arcata.

1876-1927: Arcata, California

The town in which A. W. Ericson spent almost the entire remainder of his life was situated on the northeast shore of Humboldt Bay and was one of the oldest towns in northern California. The townsite was first located in 1850, and buildings were built upon a plateau that provides an excellent view of the surrounding country. In 1860, the name of the developing community was changed from Union to an Indian word, *Arcata*, but not without mixed feelings on the part of local residents. A local newspaper, the *Times*, wrote:

"No name could be more appropriate for a village containing such sociable and fun-loving people than that of Union. Some romantic people about there, ran away with the idea that 'Arcata' is a legitimate digger [Indian] word, and means 'Union.' This is not correct. It means a certain place in town where the diggers were once in the habit of congregating, which in our language would be about the same as 'down there' or 'over yonder.' To some, 'Union' may sound as sweet by any other name, but not so with us."

Bringing with him the skills that he had gathered while employed in Trinidad, Ericson must have found the town much to his liking. It was an important shipping and supply point with a fine wharf which extended two miles into Humboldt Bay. Stands of redwood trees surrounded the site to the east, while to the west broad, fertile plains were suited to farming. For many years, the town eclipsed the now-larger community of Eureka, located about 12 miles southwest of Arcata. A town square formed a commercial and social center for the community. Known locally as the plaza, this square was surrounded on all sides by small shops and businesses.

A. W. Ericson's first order of business within the town was joining the Independent Order of Odd Fellows. Throughout the diary of his Trinidad years, constant reference was made to his fraternal ties, and it was clear that such mingling was important to him. He was employed as a telegrapher by the *North Pacific Telegraph Company.*

1877-1886: Ericson's First Store

Because A. W. Ericson's duties as a telegrapher allowed him a considerable amount of free time, and his recent experiences as part-time shop keeper for the *Trinidad Mill Company* provided him with the necessary skills, he soon opened a stationer's store in conjunction with his communications job. Following his opening, Ericson rapidly expanded his line of merchandise. In a short time, he offered for sale such diversified items as books, periodicals, school supplies, sheet music, pianos and organs, and sewing machines. Both because of his ability to make friends quickly and his wide range of services, the Ericson store gained popularity among the Arcata townspeople. With the novel addition of a reading room, or public library, it also became a gathering place for local gossip. Many of Ericson's friendships and business acquaintances that later became important to him date from the period of his first store.

1878: Marriage and Family

In June 1878, A. W. Ericson married Ella Fitzell, the daughter of a locally prominent pioneer family. After the wedding, they moved into a newly purchased home on the northern side of town, several blocks behind Ericson's store. In the years that followed, Ella gave birth to eight children, and all but one grew to adulthood. That A. W. Ericson was a great favorite to his children and grandchildren and had a fine family life, is witnessed by the childhood memories of his granddaughter, Beverly Krestensen:

> "A. W. Ericson was a very handsome man. He had blue eyes, a Van Dyke beard, and lots of curly hair — blonde in his youth and white later. He was a big man, probably about six feet tall and weighing between 190 and 200 pounds. Very vain about his clothes, he always wore a black suit, white shirt, tie and wide brimmed felt hat. As you will observe in all his pictures, he was never without the heavy watch chain and watch fob. He was pretty much of a dandy for his day, carrying a cane strictly for effect. I remember very well seeing him stride along swinging the cane with a jaunty air.
>
> "He had a wonderful personality — big, hearty laugh — which he

"Ho ye who are Heavy Laden — New baby carriages at Ericson's"

Arcata Leader
July 31, 1880

Augustus and Ella Ericson, 1878

5

used often, a great sense of humor . . . Fond of children, and liked to have me accompany him on his many trips to Eureka.

"He had a big appetite for spicy foods and liked to cook. This was his undoing as he died of a bleeding ulcer. I watched him many times cooking creamed cod fish, his favorite, and putting in whole peppercorns, which he crunched up and ate.

"His grandchildren loved him very much, and we all have wonderful memories of him — he thought we were all beautiful, handsome, and intelligent — which is every grandfather's perogative."

1882-1906: Job Printing

Although A. W. Ericson had been apprenticed to the printing trade while a young man in Orebro, he had never used his skill while in the United States. The arrival of his older brother, Richard, in August 1882 prompted him to expand his shop to include job printing. Richard was a journeyman printer, and had first learned his trade while working in Orebro's Lindska Printing Works. Later, he aided the eldest Ericson brother in his shop in Kronostadt, Russia.

The Ericsons did a wide variety of job printing tasks, including bills and invoices for local businesses, Lodge announcements and personal invitations. A wide variety of typefaces were made available to their customers. Many examples of these fonts may be found later, in the form of caption lines to A. W. Ericson's scenic views.

The Ericson presses and flats of wood block type have survived, and are sometimes used for specialty announcements by their current owner, Mr. Albert Horner of Arcata. *Southern Cross*, one of the typefaces that the Ericson brothers utilized, has won national prominence and is in general use today.

C. 1885: Early Photography

The exact date of A. W. Ericson's first interest in photography is not known. From his earliest days at Trinidad, he enjoyed a warm relationship with the young Eureka photographer, Amassa P. Flaglor, who had come to Humboldt County at the age of 21, in 1870. Flaglor soon became the area's foremost studio and portrait photographer, continuing his trade locally until 1880.

Ericson is known to have sat for a Flaglor portrait on July 13, 1872 and may have first made his acquaintance before that date. To suggest that A. W. Ericson may have been taking pictures by the above date, however, would without doubt be premature. Flaglor's photographs were taken by the so-called "wet plate" process, a cumbersome and exacting method that required the photographer to coat polished glass sheets with collodion, a mixture of gun cotton, ether and potassium iodide. Following the coating, the plate was sensitized by dipping the plate into a bath of silver nitrate solution, placed in the camera, exposed and developed while still wet; hence the name of the process. The complexity of the wet plate technique makes it seem unlikely

The Ericson residence in Arcata (top), and Richard Ericson

6

that an inexperienced amateur would have mastered this complex skill, only to let it remain unused for more than 10 years.

In December 1876, Flaglor opened a branch gallery in Arcata. Upon his arrival from Trinidad, a month later, A. W. Ericson met M. H. Grant, Flaglor's studio operator. In the course of time, a good friendship evolved between Ericson and Grant, a relationship which continued until Grant's death in 1889. Like Flaglor, Grant also photographed by the wet plate process. It seems likely that Ericson remained a photographic spectator until at least 1883.

Although various dry plate processes were used with poor success prior to 1880, the announcement of the gelatin dry plate method in that year would not have gone unnoticed by Ericson's photographer friends. Local usage of the gelatin dry plate process did not become popular for several years, and most studios relied upon wet plate methods until at least 1883. The arrival of the dry plate process in Humboldt County may well have provided A. W. Ericson with the impetus to begin taking photographs. No Ericson images have been reliably dated prior to the mid-1880's, but many contain subjects typical of that period.

The new technique eliminated many stumbling blocks for amateur photographers. No longer was it necessary for a photographer to coat his own plates and develop them while still wet and fragile. Instead, a series of photographs could be taken in relatively quick succession, to be developed at a later time. A. W. Ericson soon achieved considerable recognition for his scenic views of Humboldt County. By the end of the decade he enjoyed a reputation as the foremost landscape photographer of northern California.

1886-1889: Davies and Ericson, Druggists and Stationers

After nine years of successful business in his brick-fronted variety store, Ericson entered a partnership with J. N. Davies. Davies and Ericson located their shop on the northwest corner of Arcata's central plaza. In addition to A. W. Ericson's familiar line of stationery, books and school supplies, a wide range of drugs, patent medicines and chemicals were offered for sale. Since J. N. Davies was postmaster for Arcata, the local post office was also included within the store.

Although Ericson and Davies' store was ideally situated on one of the busiest of Arcata streets, the partnership proved a financial disaster to both men. As mortgages and debts became overdue, the business floundered. In April 1889, Ericson homesteaded the land upon which the family home was located, probably to avoid creditors. A few days later, on April 27, 1889, the partnership with Davies was dissolved. Stripped of nearly all his assets, including a number of land and timber claims that he had diligently acquired during his hard years at Trinidad, Ericson turned to his skills as a photographer for income, and soon joined in business with his brother Richard.

7

1889-1898: The Reading Room Store

During the last year of A. W. Ericson's partnership with J. N. Davies, Richard Ericson opened a confectionery store on the north side of Arcata's plaza. Although A. W. Ericson used Richard's store as a base for his photographic operations, Richard remained proprietor of the shop until 1892, when the store name changed to *A. W. & R. Ericson* and the brothers again became partners.

Because the store retained the original library, or reading room, it became popularly known as *Ericson's Reading Room Store*. It expanded to include a wide range of merchandise, including fruit, spectacles, stationery, job printing, musical instruments and Scandinavian delicacies.

1889-1917: Photography in Earnest

With the closing of the Davies and Ericson store in April 1889, A. W. Ericson began his long and most distinguished period of photography. Until 1892, he seems to have relied upon photography as his sole livelihood and traveled widely throughout Humboldt and Del Norte counties collecting images to add to his selection of scenic views. Newspapers of the day provided Arcata and Eureka readers with accounts of Ericson's travels to coastal towns and Indian villages:

> "A. W. Ericson, who has become noted for scenic photography will soon start a trip throughout the southern portion of the County taking pictures of scenery, buildings, etc. . ."
>
> *Arcata Union*, September 3, 1892

> "Among the many elegant photographic views taken by Ericson is one of the new Four Master, *Jane L. Stanford*, the largest wooden vessel ever built in California. It is a beauty, and we are pleased to state that large orders have been received for copies of the picture."
>
> *Arcata Union*, January 28, 1893

Ericson's scenic views were locally popular, and Arcata residents would eagerly await his return from a photographic foray. A few days after his return, the *A. W. & R. Ericson* storefront would display from five to twenty new scenic views, usually offered for sale at a price of 50 cents. Many Humboldt County residents decorated their homes and places of business with Ericson prints.

A. W. Ericson's photographs record the settlement of Humboldt County at a period of development unparalleled by most areas. Although he apparently plied his trade after 1885, he photographed an expanding frontier. For thousands of square miles, sparse community settlements were surrounded by untouched redwood forest. Indians commonly visited the towns. Horses and mules were the mode of transport locally on land, while schooner and steamer connected the region with the outside world.

In the course of Ericson's active years as photographer, he

"A. W. Ericson, of Arcata, who is traveling through southern Humboldt taking photographs for the World's Fair Association, photographed Hugh Smith's three immense oxen last Thursday. One of these animals weighs a little over 2,300 pounds."

Ferndale Enterprise
September 9, 1892

recorded most aspects of his area. The building of new structures, change from oxen to steam, difficulty of overland travel, bounty of farmlands, and the later arrival of modern motor cars, all provided subject matter for his camera.

Two events provided A. W. Ericson with a significant stimulus and opportunity for his photographic career. The first of these was the establishment in April 1891 of the Humboldt County Chamber of Commerce. The principle goal of this organization was to acquaint the country and world with the advantages and opportunities to be found on the redwood frontier. In pursuit of this goal, the Chamber of Commerce sponsored many promotional projects. Among them was the 1893 publication of a 112-page book, *In The Redwood's Realm.* The volume contained 126 of Ericson's scenic views and promoted national interest in the region. These photographs, accompanied by a text filled with statistics and glowing superlatives, illustrated Humboldt County's logging, ship-building, scenic vistas, railroads, homesteads, storefronts, Indians and individuals.

Even as *In The Redwood's Realm* was nearing completion, the decision was made that Humboldt County would participate in the Chicago Columbian Exposition, as an exhibitor in the California building. This important event was held during 1893, and included the best examples of the region's produce, products and assets. In the exhibit were 200 of A. W. Ericson's finest scenic views.

A. W. Ericson's views typically took the form of contact prints produced from 8- X 10-inch glass plate negatives trimmed to approximately 7 X 9 inches, although a few images from 6½- X 8½-inch and 5- X 8-inch glass plates occur. The print was usually mounted on an 11- X 14-inch, cream-colored paper board, with a typeset descriptive caption printed below the image area. Most such captions were general in nature, but a few more specific descriptions occasionally were included.

Ericson's Chicago Exposition photographs drew many favorable comments. Ironically, however, the exhibit also caused numerous difficulties for him. At the close of the fair, many exhibits were sold by the California Fair Committee to avoid the considerable expense of shipping them back to their owners in California. Among the items so auctioned were Ericson's Humboldt County photographs. In 1894, a book entitled *Our Own Country* was published, illustrated with photographs depicting scenic splendors throughout America. Among these illustrations were examples of Ericson's scenic views, credited to the *J. Manz Company* of Chicago, Illinois. Ericson received neither payment nor credit for his work. To add insult, several images were captioned as scenes thousands of miles from California. A photograph of oxen skidding giant redwood logs, for example was described as "In the forests of Arkansas."

Our Own Country was only the first instance of such misuse. Ericson complained bitterly as his work appeared time after time without payment or credit. Illustrations by A. W. Ericson were

"Don't forget when you go east to take with you some of Ericson's Fine Photographic Views of large trees, logging scenes, indians, etc., nearly 200 of which have been selected by the World's Fair Committee for exhibition at San Francisco and Chicago. . ."

Daily Standard
March 22, 1893

The Humboldt County exhibit at the Chicago Columbian Exposition of 1893.

included in many school textbooks without acknowledgement until well into current times.

Despite these disappointments, Ericson continued to be a familiar sight to Humboldt County residents, driving his buckboard and accompanied frequently by his young son Edgar. Nestled carefully in the back of the wagon, he carried his tripod-mounted Eastman 8 X 10 field camera, a bulky machine with red bellows and brass-mounted lens. To protect the camera from dust on the road, it was carried in a tight-fitting box, together with his plate holders. To guard it further from the jar and shake of the rough, backcountry roads, it was wedged securely between his tent and camping supplies, readily available for use, however, when an opportunity presented itself. He often traveled great distances to obtain his views. Such travels were of great interest to local residents, and newspapers of the day related accounts of his journeys to their readers:

> "A. W. Ericson returned from a week's trip to Hoopa Thursday. He procured a number of excellent views of the Red Headed Woodpecker and White Deerskin dances. Mr. Ericson had to pay $5.00 before he could get a picture, and then had to catch them on the jump. About 600 Indians attended, but only 60 bucks danced."
>
> *The Arcata Union,* September 16, 1893

The process of capturing an image was relatively long and cumbersome. Since the dry plates were expensive, even by today's standard, caution was necessary to assure that the image photographed was exactly as the photographer intended. Camera placement, position of human and animal subjects, direction of the light and numerous other considerations all affected the outcome.

Although dry plate photography had certain pitfalls, Ericson's photographs captured a quality sometimes missed by other photographers better versed in technique. Despite the necessity of carefully-controlled positioning of his subjects, and the near-rigid immobility that his film's insensitivity to light required, his images often retain a candid appearance. Examination of his arrangements of groups of people reveal his careful attention to detail. Within such groups, one or two individuals will be nearly always found in full profile. Such individuals became almost a trademark in Ericson's views, for they contrasted with other members to provide a careful counterpoint of attention. In such nuances A. W. Ericson excelled.

A. W. Ericson's exposure at the Columbian Exposition in Chicago had also swelled his reputation internationally. For several years after the event, he received orders for his views from publishers seeking illustrations for books on California and its Northcoast. As his name became well-known, a number of prestigious magazines included his scenic views in their editions. In its edition of February 18, 1899, the *Arcata Union* described Ericson's growing reputation:

A. W. Ericson succeeded in taking some splendid photographic views of the steamer *Pomona* as she entered the Bay last Sunday, conveying the Native Sons to Eureka. He took three pictures while the steamer was under way, he being on the Bay steamer *Silva*, which was likewise under way, the pictures are fine.

Arcata Union
April 28, 1894

10

"The February number of the *Windsor Magazine* published in London, contains . . . nine of the finest redwood photographs ever produced, and they all bear the name of our fellow citizen, A. W. Ericson, who since the exhibition of his collection at the World's Fair of 1893 has received orders from all corners of the globe for his justly celebrated views . . ."

As knowledge of A. W. Ericson's skill as a photographer became widespread, he prepared many of his views on assignment for firms and individuals. Typical of such assignments was one performed during 1893 for the *Excelsior Redwood Company.* At the company's request, he photographed all aspects of their operation: tree-felling, skidding, transport by rail, ponding of the logs, and, finally, the resultant lumber. Today, such photographic series provide a unique glimpse into early logging practices.

Because of his widespread acceptance in all levels of society, A. W. Ericson enjoyed a community relationship similar in some ways to that of the local minister or doctor. The completion of a new building, opening of a business or the excursion of a lodge frequently prompted a demand for Ericson's services.

Until about the year 1898, A. W. Ericson had printed most of his scenic views on albumen-coated paper. The process required the photographer to float the paper in a sensitizing bath of silver nitrate, then dry the stock prior to printing. Albumen prints had a soft, golden quality. Shortly before the turn of the century, however, Ericson began printing his scenic views on bromide paper, a recent innovation. The paper could be purchased pre-coated and ready-to-use. Ericson's new images were toned in a vibrant russet color, and quickly became popular.

In later years, he purchased an Eastman 8 X 10 enlarger for use in preparing enlargements of his scenic views to sizes as great as 20 X 24 inches. Such enlargements proved popular in public displays, and a number of examples have survived to the present day.

1897-1906: Portraits and Postcards

In 1897, A. W. Ericson yielded to popular request from the local citizens of Arcata and expanded his photographic efforts to include portraits. His first trial images were taken in a photo tent studio on a vacant lot near the central plaza.

His efforts as a studio portraitist prospered, and he and Richard Ericson began to search for a new store more suitable for a gallery. They eventually decided upon a site located only a few doors from their previous premises on the northeast corner of Arcata's central plaza. Unlike the preceeding variety shops, however, it offered only photography and job printing services to the public.

From his new location, A. W. Ericson continued his scenic

A. W. Ericson (front center) with a woods crew and undercut redwood tree.

"Have your stamp photo taken, you can have 28 photos with seven different positions for 25¢ at the Arcata Gallery, A. W. Ericson, proprietor."

Arcata Union
March 4, 1899

11

views, but spent a portion of each week operating the *Arcata Photograph Gallery*. His portraits were not especially outstanding examples of the art, but demonstrated the compassion with which he approached his subjects. A grandson, Robert Bryan, related:

> "Sometimes a young man would enter the studio to have a portrait made to send home to his family. The family especially wanted the picture to show how successful their young adventurer had become in his new life ... Usually, however, the young man had very little education and consequently was employed as a laborer and had only rough clothes to wear for his portrait. Ericson would outfit the subject in his own vest and coat, graced with his own precious gold watch and chain. Thus, the successful portrait would be taken."

Ericson's scenic views during this period continued to bring him the admiration of his contemporaries. In 1904, however, the photo postcard craze that had swept the nation attracted his attention, and he quickly capitalized on the popularity of the new medium by converting a large number of his scenic views to postcards. Among the most widely distributed of his scenic photographs during this period were illustrations of redwood logging and the Yurok, Hupa and Tolowa Indian tribes. Like many other studios, he also began taking postcard portraits. In their new form, his images were sent by Arcata and Eureka residents to friends and relatives around the nation and the world.

A. W. Ericson, Arcata's famous landscape photographer, was called to Vance's new camp on Wednesday to take views of a mammoth Redwood that was felled in the woods there, that morning. Niel Crowley and Ben Mattress leveled the Giant which measured 20 feet in diameter.

Arcata Union
April 29, 1899

1906: San Francisco and Monterey

By early 1906, A. W. Ericson was almost 58 years old, and several of his children were fully grown. New competition in studio photography began to reduce Ericson's business. As both Ericson brothers relied upon the shop for their sole support, a change seemed necessary. Financial opportunity is believed to have come in the form of a bequest from an unmarried man whom A. W. Ericson had befriended many years before. Leaving his brother Richard to manage the store, he departed Arcata by overland stage on April 10, 1906, bound for San Francisco. Newspaper accounts of the day make it clear that Ericson did not intend to return to Arcata, and he may have hoped to test his fortune in either San Francisco or nearby Monterey.

Arriving in San Francisco, he took a room at the *Continental Hotel* then traveled to Stockton. Since he expected to return in a few days, he asked the hotel clerk to hold his room in his absence. Upon his arrival back in San Francisco, however, he found the room had been let, and moved to another hotel, the *Cosmopolitan*. On the evening of April 17, he attended a theater with two friends, then retired to his hotel room for the night.

The following morning, at 5:12 a.m., San Francisco was rocked by one of the most destructive earthquakes of modern times. Had Ericson remained in the *Continental Hotel* he would

Ericson photographed the aftermath of the San Francisco earthquake of 1906.

surely have been injured, for a number of occupants were killed when the structure collapsed.

Dazed and shaken, A. W. Ericson wandered the streets of San Francisco throughout the ensuing fire that destroyed much of the town. During this period, he took several rolls of film with a Kodak Autographic camera. Only a few frames are memorable, however, and he was clearly affected by his turn of fortune.

In Arcata, friends and former acquaintances pondered Ericson's fate. The *Arcata Union* headlined, "Where is A. W. Ericson?" His attempt at a new start in life thwarted, A. W. Ericson returned to Arcata after a short stay in Monterey. He quickly re-established himself in the community and returned to his trade of photography.

1906-1927: A Rich Life

Upon his return to his residence in Arcata, Ericson continued his activities and again participated in many Swedish social events. He renewed his long-term association with the Independent Order of Odd Fellows and became an active member of the Lutheran Church.

A. W. Ericson with friends (top) and family a few years before his death in 1927.

A. W. Ericson's photographs from 1906 to 1917 reflect his social interests very clearly. Few major events were held without "Gus" Ericson and his familiar camera. During this period, Humboldt County's steps into the Twentieth Century were documented with the same care and precision that logging before steam and Indian dances had commanded earlier in his life. Fourth of July parades, picnics, the arrival of Humboldt's first automobiles and new store openings were all catured on film and soon appeared as displays in the Ericson store windows. After 1917, A. W. Ericson noticeably slowed his pace. Nearly 70 years of age and a grandfather several times over, he relished all aspects of his family and friends. For the first time in his busy life, he sat back, relaxed and began to reflect on his early days in Humboldt County. Total retirement, however, he still considered a pleasure for others to enjoy. Ericson set up a small photofinishing shop, run in partnership with his son Edgar and daughter Ella. The shop provided a base for his less-frequent forays. Such excursions continued until 1925, when failing health and old age made them impossible.

1927: Death at Age 79

On August 15, 1927, at the age of 79 years, Augustus William Ericson passed away in his home at Arcata. He left behind a legacy of photography unmatched by any of his nearby contemporaries. Spanning nearly 40 years, his visual record of Humboldt and Del Norte counties provides a glimpse into the history of Redwood country: its industry, people, locales and activities. During his long and productive lifetime, A. W. Ericson had developed the scenic view not only as an object of commerce but also as a historic record of his adopted homeland.

PHOTOGRAPHER OF EARLY DAY SCENES PASSES

AUGUSTUS W. ERICSON, WHO CAME HERE FROM SWEDEN 57 YEARS AGO, PASSES AT ARCATA HOME MONDAY AFTER SHORT ILLNESS. FIRST WORKED IN WOODS AT TRINIDAD AND LATER ENGAGED IN BUSINESS IN ARCATA. MADE A REPUTATION AS PHOTOGRAPHER.

Notes about the Plates

While images taken by A. W. Ericson appear frequently in a wide variety of public and private collections, only the Humboldt State University library has significant numbers of original negatives. Other collections normally include original prints, copy negatives, copy prints, or a combination of all three forms. Of the nearly 575 known original negatives which have survived, perhaps 80% exist as 8- by 10-inch glass plates. The remaining 20% include 6½- by, 8½-, 5- by 8-, and 3½- by 5-inch glass plates, as well as approximately 60 flexible, roll-film negatives.

Because no extensive effort has been made to compile a directory of existent images, it is difficult to assess and provide precise information as to the probable number of surviving original Ericson prints. Following several years of personal search, the author is frequently contacted by individuals who hold private collections of early photographs. On many such occasions, new original Ericson prints are identified. Throughout the region where Ericson was active, and with increasing regularity in other areas, this process continues to reveal new aspects and viewpoints of his work. The interested cooperation of private holders has greatly aided the author's efforts to locate, identify and obtain file negatives of Northern California's regional photographs.

The condition and quality of the negatives and original prints thus discovered vary from examples of near-pristine quality to those which exhibit extensive damage through misuse, scratching, abrading, solarization, mildew or simple aging. Many images have been stored without substantial protection of any sort, and in the case of glass plate negatives, breakage has been common. When such negatives are not also available in the form of original prints, they have been irretrievably lost.

While many fine Ericson original prints have been treasured as family heirlooms, and were carefully framed and displayed, others have been destroyed through the uncaring attitudes of those who did not recognize their worth. A happening which occured during the author's search and in which original prints were destroyed, exemplifies such hazards. In this case, more than 20 Ericson original prints were discovered on a local sidewalk following an overnight exposure to rainshowers. These images had been discarded by a family during their move to a new residence and, although several previously unknown photographs were included all were damaged beyond retrieval.

Two similar stories are common with regard to glass plates. A rumor which circulates through Ericson's home town suggests that a greenhouse may have been constructed from a number of his original glass plates in the years following his death. Proof of the existence of such a building has not been determined, however, and the story remains unsubstantiated. In a second instance, two boxes containing about 360 Ericson glass plates (including many of those used in the portfolio section of this book) owe their survival to an unknown passerby. This unrecognized patron rescued the negatives from an alleyway behind the Ericson shop after they had been discarded, pending removal to the local dump. By returning the boxes to the store, he prompted their subsequent storage.

Original prints frequently exhibit a wide range of physical characteristics. Many glass plates were printed repeatedly by Ericson, over a period of many years. These prints reflect changing technical trends, styles, and Ericson's response to the taste of the purchasing public. Individual image tones span the spectrum from a pale, yellow-cream to a deep russet, depending upon the printing process Ericson employed, their toning and subsequent aging characteristics. Through the years these scenic views have been alternately stored in chests or attics out of the reach of light, or subjected to grime, abrasion, and other abuses of ill-care.

In addition to more common physical forms, Ericson frequently produced photographs for use as postcards. Ericson portraits reproduced in this medium are especially common, and may frequently be found in local collections dating later than 1904. Scenic views that have been converted to postcards usually show evidence of extreme cropping as they were often contact printed portions of larger negatives. Because of this factor, most do not accurately represent the original scenic views. After World War I, postcard scenic views were commonly reproduced in greater volume by offset lithography.

Finally, a sizeable number of periodicals, journals, and books contain examples of Ericson's photographic efforts. Many interesting illustrations of his work are known today only in this form, unfortunately not suitable for further reproduction. More rarely, Ericson images were reproduced on silk, photo buttons, calendar illustrations, and as large, glass magic-lantern slides. A few hand-colored original prints exist, but the coloring of such images was probably not done by Ericson.

The images selected for reproduction in the portfolio section of this book should not be construed to represent all aspects of A. W. Ericson's photographic efforts. Examples of his many portraits are one obvious omission. Those scenic views chosen were selected in an attempt to aid the reader's understanding of Ericson's most forceful period of work. They also represent a wide spectrum of interests, and depict his distinctive awareness of subject matter. Because the selection was, in part, limited by space, many equally deserving views have been necessarily excluded. For instance, Ericson's diverse redwood images alone might well provide the basis for another book dealing specifically with early logging.

When possible, reproductions included in the portfolio section were obtained from original negatives. The remainder were generated from original Ericson prints, or copy negatives from their original prints. Every effort was made to assure consistency in cropping with Ericson's own examples, although no precedent existed in some cases. Limited reconstruction of damaged or time-worn photographs has been undertaken only when scratches,

15

gouges, or other abuse interfered significantly with appreciation of the image itself.

Dating the images has been an area of difficulty, as A. W. Ericson made no effort to edge date his plates, and only occasionally provided dates in captions for original prints. Frequently all that may be said about an image's date or origin is that it was taken before a certain time, such as the 1893 publication of *In The Redwoods Realm.* Other significant mileposts that provided date information include newspaper accounts of Ericson's travels, introduction of bromide printing paper, advent of the photo postcard, and the respective ages of Ericson's familiar subjects, including family members. No attempt has been made to include the earliest or latest known examples of his work.

To aid the reader in understanding the uniqueness of the region in which A. W. Ericson was active, the captions appearing with the photographs in the portfolio section have been amplified to provide background information of interest. It is the author's hope that the included images will provide a provocative glimpse into life in an early era, and a thoughtful awareness of the photographic vision of Augustus William Ericson.

Portfolio

From earliest times in California history, the attention of botanist and casual onlooker alike has been drawn by the legend of the coast redwoods. Visitors to the area stood in amazed wonder at the size and breadth of these forest giants.

In A. W. Ericson's forty years of active photography, he recorded the changing face of an expanding frontier. Man and animal power quickly passed to that of machine before the watchful eye of his camera. Joined to the outside world by intercoastal sailing ship and steamer, travel within Humboldt County was slow and arduous. Mule, horse, and foot travel linked the growing community centers. Here, a pack train of 55 mules leaves the *A. Brizard Company* in Arcata, enroute inland to Hoopa, a town 50 miles distant.

20

Oxen teams numbering 16 to 20 animals were a common sight in northern California lumber camps until nearly 1895, as they pulled giant redwood logs from the forests along skid roads made of small, green logs. Each ox pair, known as a span, could pull more than 4,000 pounds. Log sections over 10 feet in diameter and weighing up to 40 tons were not uncommon. Oak barrels were placed at the edge of the skid road, providing a source of water or tallow to reduce friction between the sliding logs and the roadbed.

Throughout the northwest, loggers succumbed to the notion that a man was not a woodsman until "he had a dollar watch and his picture taken in front of a tree." Itinerant photographers took many such pictures, and local papers were crowded with the announcements of their arrival. Resident photographers were also a common sight around the woods camps. Among the latter, A. W. Ericson became widely-known to Californians for his scenic views of rugged men and sturdy tools posed before doomed giants of the forest.

With the advent of steam, the redwood logs were transported from the woods landing over short, company railroads such as those shown in this scenic view. The *Excelsior Redwood Company* with operations in Freshwater, California owned several locomotives by 1892, when this view was probably taken. A. W. Ericson traveled throughout the area taking photographs for display at the Chicago Columbian Exposition of 1893. These trains were especially loaded for this purpose.

Arcata, California was the community chosen by Ericson for his permanent home in the years following his arrival from Sweden and short employment at Trinidad. Situated on a wide plain near Humboldt Bay, its fine wharf made it an ideal gateway to redwood country.

Many of A. W. Ericson's photographs show the communities and people of northcoast California. A wide diversity of economic factors drew settlers to the area, and the industries of lumbering, shipbuilding, farming, livestock raising, and mining were quickly established.

Because Ericson's photographs span nearly four decades in the development of the frontier, they recorded a profile of this progress. Citizens long dead and children now grown to old age are preserved through the thoughtful memory of his photographs. A. W. Ericson's images

do not provide answers to questions regarding why settlement took place. Instead, they show how these acts were accomplished. The results of his interest in photography have been judged important not because his photographs were as good or better than those of his contem-

poraries, but because he documented a region and a people at an important stage in their development.

25

Among the most famous of A. W. Ericson's photographs are those which depict the Indians common to northern California. Anthropological collections of many major museums are indebted to him for their images of everyday native life. Among such photographs is this view, showing an Indian spearing for salmon in a river near present-day Hoopa. The situation is obviously posed, for Indians of the Hupa tribe made extensive use of weirs in securing their catches of salmon. In spite of this, photographs such as these excited the imaginations of many 19th century Americans.

Much of the region consisted of virgin redwood forests. Because of the crude methods employed prior to the introduction of the Dolbeer steam donkey, however, only the most accessible trees were harvested. Many Ericson images show the grandeur of the forest primeval. In taking such pictures he was handicapped by the insensitivity of his film to light. Although the gelatin dry plate process which he used was a great improvement over earlier wet plate techniques, exposures were still long. In addition, the film was principally sensitive to blue light, such as that from the unclouded sky. This, in combination with optical flare caused by the lenses then available, served to obscure much skyline detail, and may be responsible for the sunlight-like shafts of light seen in this image.

27

The coastal port of Trinidad was A. W. Ericson's first residence in far northern California. Built in the years of the gold rush, the town's history already stretched back nearly 75 years to its discovery by the Bruno de Hezeta sea exploration of 1775. It prospered for a few years after the gold fields dwindled, and Ericson found it a lively company town of the *Trinidad Mill Company*. He worked in the logging trade until 1876, when he relocated to Arcata. After his interest in photography began, he returned on occasion to record its changing face with his camera. This scenic view was probably taken between 1888 and 1892.

One of the central features of Trinidad was its wharf, thrusting into the sea along a jutting headland. Coastal vessels, both sail and steam, loaded finished lumber and other products for San Francisco and other ports around the world. Smaller vessels, such as the steamer above, also called on "doghole" ports to receive their cargo of lumber. In many cases, these lading points could scarcely be called ports at all, and consisted of rocky coves, lees behind small islands, or partially sheltered water found behind sawtoothed reefs. Frequently, loads of lumber were hoisted aboard the vessels through systems of elaborate booms and high leads that caused many anxious moments for the ship's master and crew. Thus, the momentary safety of a true port, such as Trinidad, was appreciated by the coastal traders.

Inland from the seacoast, villages and towns quickly grew along major trade routes. Throughout the west both streams and trails provided avenues for commerce, but in northern California, the redwood forests yielded in the valleys to more easily cleared trees and shrubs. Soon, clusters of farm buildings and acres of tilled land dotted the alluvial river terraces. Churches and stores added to the growing construction. By 1893, Humboldt County had grown to a population of 26,579, mostly due to the expansion of small communities.

Transportation, in the early days, consisted of horse, horse and buggy, mule, or simply travel by foot. Many Sundays were highlighted by a buggy ride to visit friends and acquaintances.

Beginning with the gold rush, the forests echoed first to the sound of axes and saws, and later to the footsteps of towns-people. Dandies and laborers vied for a place in the many photographs taken of partially-cut giants. Due to the immense size of the trees, they could not be climbed through use of the customary rope and leather tech-niques. Instead, choppers cut deep notches, into which long, iron-tipped hardwood planks, or springboards, could be insert-ed. A series of such springboards provided a base upon which to stand while the cutting took place and enabled the logger to begin his cut well above the wide portion of the trunk where the tree entered the ground.

Resting in jaws of questionable safety, these loggers take a break from their labors before continuing the backcut which eventually felled the tree shown. The length of time necessary for two men to fall a redwood varied according to the size of the tree, but could take as long as three or four days. The efforts necessary to bring a redwood to earth were backbreaking, and depended on giant tools such as the long-handled axe pictured at the lower right of the photograph.

33

The white deerskin dance, also known as the summer and along-the-river dance, was held biennially in September by natives of the Trinity and Klamath rivers. Frequently, the activities would last for several days, traveling up-river from village to village until hundreds of Indians were involved. In the afternoon of the third day, the so-called "boat dance" began, floating down the river to the oak forests near present-day Redwood National Park.

Only men participated in the white deerskin dance, clad in highly-prized clothing made of albino deerskin. A. W. Ericson became famous for his photographs of the dance, for his pictures of the Indians were circulated widely throughout the United States. During cere- monies such as the white deer- skin dance, a white man's pres- ence was often viewed by the Indians as a nuisance, and more than once Ericson was required to pay a model's fee of five dollars to take pictures. Even so, his scenic views were often blurred by the motion of his uncooperative subjects.

Ericson's scenic views frequently recorded scenes of popular whimsy, such as this group resting at roadside beneath a fire-hollowed redwood tree with the legend "Hotel Sequoia." Although protected from all but the most severe forest fires by their thick fibrous bark, *Sequoia Sempervirens* skinned by windfalls frequently became hollowed by dry rot and fire. In earlier, pioneer days, such trees had been used by settlers as temporary pens for livestock and were locally known as "goosepen trees."

Moonstone Beach, located 12 miles northwest of Arcata, became a popular spot for picnickers in search of clams, mussels and crab. At this point, the wide, sandy beaches and hummocky dunes yielded to rocky shores upon which the residents could search for "moonstones," a milky form of agate marked with a white or yellow crescent.

With development of Humboldt Bay as a seaport, an active ship-building industry was soon under way. The barkentine *Hilo* was one of many ships launched into the bay at *Bendixson's Ship-yards,* and was destined for the coastal lumber trades between San Francisco and Portland.

The men who labored on the logging railroads were a sturdy lot, used to long hours and meager pay. Frequently, the locomotives were as tired and hard-driven as the men who worked them. As many as 50 steam engines puffed and whistled on the grades and trestles of Humboldt and Del Norte counties between 1890 and 1915, carrying loads ever increasing distances to the mills as the lumber camps receded from the towns.

Stimulated by a climate of mild, moist winters and long, moderate summers, huge crops of wheat and potatoes rewarded the farmers' efforts in the river valleys and bottomlands near Arcata. Farm implements designed for use behind horses appear unusual today, but were both functional and efficient by the standards of the early days.

The barkentine *Jane L. Stanford* (left) was among the largest of vessels built at the shipyards across the bay from Eureka. Many dignitaries were present for its launching in 1892, and probably were carried from Arcata and Eureka by the bay ferries that provided much of the area's transport.

The great contrast in Indian lifestyles may be easily seen by
comparing the pictures on these
pages with those found in other
sections of the portfolio. A. W.
Ericson titles the brave at left
"Kah-hah," and his leathery face,
legs and feet reveal the hardships
of native life in the region. "Kah-
hah" was probably from the
Hupa tribe, and lived in a village
along the Trinity River. His appearance and dress differ widely
from the women shown at right,

42

but both reveal the extent of
white influence on the natives.
The Victorian-style dresses and
bright, "Indian" blankets were
as foreign to Indians of northern
California as the smock-like
garment worn at left.

Eureka, California in the early days was reminiscent of many present-day motion picture settings, with its wide, unpaved streets, wooden sidewalks, and false-fronted stores. The banner at upper right announced the arrival of the Native Sons of the Golden West's excursion. Eureka was a popular destination of lodges and fraternal organizations seeking an unusual weekend convention. From the city, they would frequently take one-day side trips to the redwood forests and beaches, or toured the bay on a sternwheel ferry.

The residence of William Carson, an early lumber baron, was a fitting standard by which all Victorian architecture might be judged. Colorfully decorated with a red shingle roof with tin flashings, the top cupola provided Carson a vantage point from which he could view both his sawmill and the lumber schooners that entered the bay. The grounds were not yet fully landscaped in this view taken before 1890, but palm trees, rose gardens, and colorful seasonal flowers soon added grace to Eureka's finest home. The Carson mansion has survived the tests of time and declining fortunes, and is today a private men's club.

Travel to points south of Eureka depended for many years on the grace of the Eel River, a wide stream named for its abundant spawning runs of lamprey eels. By 1868, however, the cross-river ferry at Dungan Pool pro-vided a safer, more dependable method of transportation over the stream. This scenic view was taken much later, when the ferry traffic had already been reduced by a seasonal bridge made of pontoon floats.

The courthouse of Klamath County doubled as a school for many years after the governmental district became a part of Del Norte, Humboldt, and Trinity counties in 1874. With the coming of the photographer, children were dutifully arranged into neat rows, and the schoolmistress stood proudly with her charges for an official portrait. Ericson repeated this scene at many schoolhouses of the area.

Felling of a redwood began with the labor of two men who alternately chopped, then sawed the tree, in a process lasting several days. While the tree was being cut, preparation for its fall was made by other workmen, who built a bed of boughs trimmed from previously-fallen trees to ease its impact. Because redwood is quite brittle, many trees were left in the woods by early-day loggers after they shattered. Modern felling techniques have greatly reduced this problem, and the scenes of destruction that once were common are, for the most part, a thing of the past.

Teams of oxen or horses pulled
logs from the woods to a landing
or railhead. The team of horses
above is dwarfed by the log in
the foreground, and it provides
a graphic means of understanding
the enormous size of redwood
timber.

The photographer became his own subject in this scenic view taken about 1892. A. W. Ericson is seated on the cut section at the center of the image, his prized gold watch fob, emaculate beard, and necktie clearly show- ing. Unlike many of his competitors, Ericson seldom had his photograph taken, and no views depict his cameras or other equipment. When shown, he always appears nattily dressed, sometimes in stark contrast to his associates.

Dwarfed by a field of giant logs, the two men at right center provide scale to this logging scene, probably taken in northern Humboldt County. In the five year period beginning in 1888, nearly eight million board feet of redwood lumber were harvested. Huge quantities of shingles, shakes, pickets, posts, lathes, doors, mouldings, window frame stock, and cord wood were also produced, most destined for shipment out of the area. In many cases, the sites of forest scenes such as that shown above today are clothed in copious second growth trees, and many acres of once-cutover land are now preserved in state and national parks.

With the advent of the Dolbeer steam donkey, the flavor of the woods crews changed from a dependence on horses and oxen to that of shrill whistles, and singing wire and rope cables. Logs were yarded from the woods to landings, then transported by trains to the mills. Tall trees on the ridge tops were often bent to service as poles for "high lead" logging, and the sight of huge redwood logs flying along the ground became common. The use of steam greatly extended the range of the cutters, and opened the forests to the saw in many previously inaccessible areas.

A. W. ERICSON

52

John Vance's lumber mill on Mad River was typical of sawmill operations during the 1880's. The mill was serviced by a company train and logging rail that not only brought cut logs from the woods, but transported the finished lumber to a shipping point at the seacoast. Stacks of rough-finished lumber stood in the open drying yards, and company towns, complete with bunkhouses, stores, cook houses, and rude homes sprouted in the newly-cleared forests.

53

The lighthouse at Trinidad, California was constructed in 1871 on a rocky headland nearly 100 feet above the water of the Pacific Ocean. Because of the view obtainable from its heights, the lighthouse became a popular spot for visitors to Trinidad. In 1897, a large bell was added to the lighthouse to aid in warning coastal shipping away from the sawtooth reefs found a short distance offshore. With these precautions, Trinidad became a popular harbor that provided protection from the strong northerly winds common to the region in summer.

A short distance north of Trinidad, a wide body of water known as Big Lagoon divided the mouth of Maple Creek from the nearby ocean. The spot was popular for duck hunters, campers, and, in later days, picnickers.

In addition to the farmlands of the region, livestock were a common feature of redwood country ranches. Both sheep and cattle were raised in the hill country to the east of Arcata on the Angel Ranch. In the early days of the area, Angel Ranch was a convenient stopping point for pack trains of mules that carried supplies many miles inland from the seacoast to rural stores and trading posts.

With the introduction of dairy cattle, small creameries were built to fill the needs of the farmers for a place where milk could be gathered for conversion to butter. Such creameries were a common sight throughout northern California's rich dairy lands. A. W. Ericson identified the business above as *The Arcata Creamery,* and it was probably located in the flat bottomlands below that city.

The redheaded woodpecker, or jump, dance was performed by Indians of Weitchpec, California in the years between the white deerskin dance. The natives were clad for the dance in ceremonial clothing that included unique headdresses made of the feathers of the redheaded woodpecker, necklaces of dentalium shell money, loin robes of deerskin, and rattles that were woven from native grasses. A. W. Ericson traveled widely to obtain many of his Indian views, sometimes camping for as much as a week. He was joined at the celebrations by other white men, many of whom took an active interest in the native gatherings.

Captain John, a chief of the Hupa clan, often posed for Ericson's camera. Northwestern California Indians did not have formal tribes such as those common in the midwestern United States; rather, they lived in extended family groups. Captain John was a member of the Med-ildin Rancheria, and was an active chief for more than 40 years. In 1858, while still a young man, he was taken by the whites to San Francisco. The purpose of the trip was to show him how many white people were located there, probably to discourage uprisings such as those which had occurred previously from time to time. By the time this picture was taken, he was an old man, probably more than 60 years of age. The structure behind him is a sweathouse, a popular feature of many Indian villages.

59

From the time that he established his first store in 1877, A. W. Ericson took frequent trips to San Francisco to order merchandise and visit business acquaintances. The Cliff House, perched precariously above the Pacific Ocean, was a familiar sight to him. The structure seen in this scenic view was the second such building to occupy the site; the first burned down a few years earlier. In the course of many years of such visits, he acquired a great fondness for the city. When one of his daughters was afflicted with deafness, she attended a private school there that specialized in children with hearing problems.

In nearby Golden Gate Park, ornate buildings and careful landscaping provided a respite from the hustle and bustle of the business district. Ericson does not identify the group near the center of the frame, but the two feminine figures are probably his daughters.

The *Excelsior Redwood Company* controlled and owned 10,000 acres of redwood timber at Freshwater, California. Included in this land were thousands of acres of virgin redwoods, many trees of which were of great size. In preparation for the Chicago Columbian Exposition, the company cut several huge trees and loaded them aboard the flatcars of the *Eureka and Freshwater Railroad.* Ericson was called to the scene to photograph these trains for a display in the California exhibit, and many visitors to the World's Fair were awed by the forest giants recorded in his scenic views.

A few years after this picture was taken, negotiations began for the eventual sale of the *Excelsior Redwood Company* to a combine of the *Santa Fe Land and Improvement Company* and the *Murphy Syndicate.* Frank Murphy abandoned his copper mining interests in Arizona and traveled west to begin a long career in timber and lumber. With Hiram Smith as president and Murphy as vice-president, the newly-named *Freshwater* *Lumber Company* soon grew to become *The Pacific Lumber Company,* the world's largest redwood firm.

With the falling of a great tree, the task of bucking it into sections small enough for transport began. The members of the bucking crew labored from dawn to dusk at the end of large saws, or "misery whips." On many occasions, their work was made more difficult by the position of a tree. When problems such as this occurred, the sawyers would curse their lot with good reason, for it was often necessary for them to cut for an hour or more on their hands and knees before the task could be completed.

Pride of the woods crew was the operator of the steam donkey. Because of the remote location of many cutting sites, these men were responsible for watering, fueling, relocating and repairing their often-balky machines. Equipped with winches of tremendous power, the steam donkey pulled itself into the woods when the operator attached its cable to a standing tree, then hauled cut logs from the felling site to the railroad landings. Many operators were killed or maimed during these operations, for the strain was great on both the winch and cable. When either failed, the ensuing whiplash of flying steel was easily capable of severing a limb or snapping bones.

The *Arcata and Mad River Railroad* inspection car, shown at left, was one of a long series of vehicles employed to travel the nearly two-mile long Arcata Wharf. The railroad had only been in existance for a few months when its first accident occurred, in early October, 1855. On that occasion, the "locomotive jumped the track and broke her right hind leg." By comparison, the train upon which the company superintendent, Victor Zaruba, is seated had a long and useful career.

66

With completion of the Arcata Wharf, much of the shipping traffic into Humboldt Bay called on Arcata for lumber from the area's abundant mills. Over 100 ships per year visited the facility by 1892, more than half bound for foreign ports. The small steam vessel at right was probably the *Ada*, and was one of the three bay ferries in active service at the time. These sternwheelers called on towns, road landings, and lumber mills, carrying on a bay commerce that remained active until recent years.

Large, hydraulic nozzles, or monitors, replaced gold pans and cradles in the years following the gold rush as the precious yellow metal became more difficult to mine. These scenes were taken near Orleans, California at the Jonas Salstrom and William Lord mines. Unlike the hand methods, monitor mining took a terrible toll of land and topsoil, and erosion from early mining operations clouded the rivers with sediment.

Chinese laborers provided much of the manpower necessary to keep the hydraulic mines operating. They built dams high on the hillside creeks to provide sufficient water pressure to keep the huge "water cannons" flowing. After an area had been washed for an hour or more, they piled the rocks which emerged into huge, pyramid-like structures so that mining could continue. Many such rockpiles remain today.

Since the Klamath River crossing at Martin's Ferry was a scenic, peaceful spot when Ericson recorded his view of the Bald Hills Road, the time of year was likely mid-summer. If he had returned in mid-winter, his camera would have revealed a swollen river, sometimes high enough to reach the cable seen above the ferry. At such times, the region became impassable, and settlers were content to remain by their firesides.

North Fork Falls, a rocky stretch of the Mad River approximately 8 miles east of Arcata, was a popular fishing spot in Ericson's time. During fall spawning runs, salmon and steelhead ascended the stream to lay eggs in the river gravel below the falls, but the climb through the jagged rocks and swift water stopped all but the hardiest. At such times, anglers equipped with steelhead flies, as well as less sporting individuals carrying pitchforks, would descend on the stream, for the fish were frequently so crowded in the pools below the falls that it was a simple task to catch a barrelful. In depiction of out-of-the-way spots such as Martin's Ferry and North Fork Falls, A. W. Ericson distinguished himself from his fellow photographers, who seldom left the main roads and towns in search of pictures.

71

Both the picture above and that opposite were taken at the shake and shingle claim of "Oley" C. Hansen. A claim such as Hansen's could provide a comfortable living for the owner and his employees, as redwood shingles, shakes, and shake bolts were in great demand for the roofing of houses. Many trees of prime redwood fell for this purpose in the earliest days, and a man could cut one tree, spend a year or more breaking it into shakes, raft them to a nearby port, and

sell them at sufficient profit to live happily for several years to come. The work was dangerous, however, as were all woods jobs. In times of wind, dead branches popularly called "widow-makers" were a constant hazard to the men. Falling from a height of 250 feet or more, such limbs could stun or kill. It was considered a good cutting season indeed if less than 20 men were killed or crippled in the woods.

This view shows an Indian family in the hills near Hoopa, California. By the turn of the century, many natives had adopted the ways of the white men, but were still drawn to age-old traditions such as the basket cradle held by the woman at right. In such baskets, a child was bound tightly in a blanket, so that only his legs were free to kick. Often, children remained in the cradle until nearly three years of age. Note also the distinctive headgear worn by the woman. A tightly-woven basket marked with a design was a common feature of the Hupa tribe, and seldom were their women seen without this basket "hat."

Taken at the site of Fort Gaston in the Hoopa Valley, the Indian people shown above were awaiting the distribution of rations. Following a miners' massacre in the late 1850's, a reservation was established at Hoopa, and the Indians were administered by the Bureau of Indian Affairs and a contingent of soldiers at Fort Gaston. Because the reservation was unable to support the natives, they recieved a ration of food supplies from the government long after the fort had been abandoned. Fort Gaston was also the site of the *A. Brizard Company* trading post and was an important stop until well after 1900 for company mule trains.

On April 27, 1894, the Grand Lodge, Native Sons of the Golden West excursion visited the region of Korbel, and had their picture taken atop a redwood stump nearly 22 feet in diameter. Such excursions were common, and visited many areas of the county. Newspaper accounts of the day indicated that the "excursionists seemed in the best of spirits," probably the result of copious imbibing while enroute to their destination.

When redwood trees became weakened by rot or the soil surrounding their roots was saturated with water, strong winds could topple the giants. Such was the fate of the tree pictured below, brought to earth not by the efforts of men and their axes, but the forces of nature. In mature, virgin forests, hundreds of fallen trees littered the forest floor. They presented a stumbling block of gargantuan proportions to early explorers, who recorded in their journals with frustration a day's progress of less than one-half mile.

Not far from the center of town, this rural scenic view depicted early suburban lifestyles. Only a few years prior to this photograph, the area had been redwood forest, and one stump that remained after cutting may be seen at lower right. With the expansion of the community, white frame houses began to dot the hillsides northeast of Arcata as men claimed the land from the forests.

Few rural schoolhouses in America could boast of a giant stump playground upon which to enjoy a rousing game of "King of the Mountain" like this one. A. W. Ericson frequently took advantage of these natural features in posing subjects for group portraits, and many of his views retain their charm even today. While schools were first constructed in the communities bordering Humboldt Bay, they soon followed the settlers eastward in their expansion.

Adjacent to the town of Trinidad where A. W. Ericson spent his first years, was a rocky beach with scenic headlands. He spent many hours combing the beach for shells and mussels. The scenic view above captures a group of girls, possibly Ericson's daughters, walking the tideline of this rugged spot.

The Battery Point lighthouse was located a short distance offshore of Crescent City, California. Crescent City was located nearly 70 miles north of Ericson's home of Arcata, and this view appears to mark the northern extent of his travels in search of photographs. In journeying to the site, Ericson passed over unpaved road for many miles, crossed the Klamath River and Redwood Creek by ferry, and spent nearly three days enroute. Today, the distance may be traveled by automobile in less than two hours.

Logs such as those pictured above frequently weighed more than 40 tons apiece, and were called "butt cuts" in description of the portion of the tree from which they were taken. The massive log in the foreground prob- ably had a diameter of 12 feet, and was dwarfed by other trees taken from the woods by earlier loggers. Some stumps found in redwood country measured over 20 feet in diameter, more than a third larger than the cut shown here. Even modern trucks with a load capacity of 20 tons are incapable of carrying trees of such great size. When faced with large butt cuts, the logs are usu- ally split in half with a single section forming the load.

This view records an interesting sidelight of redwood logging. The 19th century millionaire William Waldorf Astor once made a $25,000 wager with an English gentleman, General Williams, that "he could seat 27 guests around a table made from a single cross section of a great California redwood tree." Astor placed his order with the *John Vance Mill and Lumber Company,* and a tree was selected and cut on Lindsay Creek. It provided a clear section over 15 feet in diameter and three feet thick. After shipment around Cape Horn in 1897, the polished slab of redwood provided a sumptuous base for a dinner party and decided the bet. Unfortunately for Astor, the cost of acquiring his table was nearly as great as the amount he won.

With the approach of the turn of the century, bicycles became an object of great interest, for they provided both utility and recreation in traveling moderate distances. The Arcata bicycle club was a popular organization, and one will note that their outings were well attended. In preparation for this picture, several of the club's more agile members climbed the tree at center with their two-wheel steeds and rested comfortably upon its branches.

In a similar manner, game hunting provided both food and recreation for early residents of northern California. From left to right, Lee Wiley, Rastus Dickerson, Rease Wiley, Walter Wiley, and "Ack" Garcelon pose with their wet dogs and a day's take of ducks.

The changing influence of time on the Indians of Arcata is clearly evident in this picture of a half-breed family. The woman clearly retains the customary tattoo marks about her chin that were considered both an object of utility and beauty. Because additional lines were added with the passage of time and with her increase in tribal standing, it was once easy to tell the age and status of many coastal Indian women. Because many of the practitioners of tattooing developed blood poisoning after receiving new marks, the whites soon outlawed the tradition.

Ericson titled his image of basket weaving, "Mad River Annie." Although this photograph was probably taken after 1900, the baskets that she is shaping are traditional to the area. The largest of these, seen at right, is the burden basket and was used for carrying wood. The three baskets to her left were (clockwise from top) a meal tray, sifting basket used in the making of acorn soup, and a carrying basket to hold white grass used in her weaving. Note the patterns on the carrying basket. Mad River Annie lived for part of the year in the sand dunes near the mouth of Mad River, for many of the reeds and grasses needed for weaving grew at that site.

Stretching north from Arcata, the lines of the *Little River Railroad Company* crossed a series of stream valleys on trestles made of "spiles," large piles driven into the ground for the support of track timbers. The crossing shown was particularly difficult, and a tall, single-spile trestle was constructed over 100 feet above the surrounding terrain. When completed, the trestle bore the weight not only of the train and its cars, but thousands of board feet of redwood timber.

The *Oregon and Eureka Railroad* was an anchronism of its type. Its locomotives traveled neither to Eureka nor Oregon, nor did it own the rails over which they traveled. Despite these limitations, it had an active, useful life from 1903 to 1911. Engine number 11 was the pride of the line, a 2-8-0 of massive proportions, and was later owned by the *Hammond Lumber Company*. Here, it crosses the Luffenholtz trestle burdened with more than 20 carloads of logs.

Because of A. W. Ericson's active community ties, he was a good friend to many shopkeepers, and visited them often during his travels about Eureka and Arcata.

With the opening of new facilities, remodeling, or simply at the owners' request, Ericson would take photographs of the businesses. The drygoods shop shown below belonged to *Seely and Titlow,* and was located near

Ericson's shop in Arcata. A true general merchandise, the store offered a wide variety of items that ranged from canned foods and clothing to seeds and laundry soap. The tracked ladders were an aid in obtaining items from their tall shelves.

Next door to Ericson's Arcata photograph gallery, *J. C. Bull's* butcher shop offered the finest in cut meats, bacon, hams and sausages. The ornate iron decorations seen at left were useful for hanging sides of pork and legs of mutton prior to cutting, for the butcher frequently cut meat to the order of his customer. The practice assured both quality and freshness, as well as client satisfaction.

A. W. ERICSON

The *Oregon and Eureka* steam engine number 11 shown above is the same 2-8-0 found on page 89. This scenic view was probably taken soon after the locomotive was delivered to the railroad, for the machine is a picture of neatness with its iron and brass highly polished. Engines such as number 11 held tremendous quantities of water and, when fully fired, was capable of moving huge loads. During the 1960's, this locomotive was donated to the City of Eureka by *Georgia-Pacific Corporation*, who acquired it from *Hammond Lumber Company* when they purchased the Hammond facilities. It is on display at the Eureka City Park.

Typical of the roads, found in rural northern California was this view of U. S. Highway 101 at Princess Rock north of Arcata. Note the carriage and horse at lower right center in the picture. Such roadways were maelstroms of powder-fine dust in summer, and quagmires of mud in winter. Deep ruts and blown down trees were a common feature throughout the year, and progress was often slow. By 1903, however, the highway was extended south to San Francisco, and overland stages plied the routes between roadhouses sometimes questionable in quality and service.

The Isaac Minor quarry was a monument to the dedication of a single man. Minor, nearing the end of his life and wealthy beyond his needs, imported Italian quarrymen to Humboldt County to split and section the huge granite boulder shown above for use in the construction of his mausoleum. To provide transport for the stone from the quarry to the cemetery to Arcata, a special railroad spur was added to the *Arcata and Mad River Railroad,* and the huge blocks of stone were shipped to the construction site. Upon completion of the edifice, Minor survived the burial of many of his kin, only to die on a trip outside the area. He is believed to be the only member of his family not buried in the tomb.

A giant of a different sort, this stump was a favorite subject for the camera of A. W. Ericson, the lone figure shown above. Taken in about 1908, Ericson was over 55 years of age at the time. The setting was one of Ericson's favorites, particularly when photographing group pictures such as that on page 79.

Sunny Grove Ranch, the property of William Duse, was another favorite subject of Ericson. Probably because of his close friendship with the owner, a number of fine views depict life on the ranch. Duse's chicken house, shown below, was a wonder throughout the region's agricultural community. It was 90 feet long, 16 feet wide, and two stories high, and housed hundreds of white leghorn chickens like the rooster displayed in the foreground.

With the passage of time, Ericson turned more and more to people-centered subject matter. This development in his scenic views was undoubtedly a result of the time he spent with portraiture. In the scene above, Mr. J. H. Bloemer, the proprietor of the *Union Laundry Company*, poses with his crew in front of his premises. Starting early in the day, Bloemer would make his rounds of Arcata to collect soiled linens and garments to be washed. By mid-morning, he would have returned to the laundry, where the washing, rinsing, and drying on outdoor lines took place. Frequently, satisfied customers would receive their wash, neatly bundled and folded, by early evening.

Because of frequent summer fog, it was not uncommon for entire families to travel inland to camp in a warmer climate. Such encampments would frequently include both grandmothers and newborn babies, often lasting for more than a month. Note the pet fawn at lower right in the picture above.

A. W. ERICSON

The great outdoors provided a diversity of interests to vacationing city residents. Besides the healthful living to be obtained by living in the fresh air, hiking, fishing, hunting, and gathering fruits and berries occupied much of their time. When rainstorms enforced idleness, the time was filled with storytelling, singing, or other group activities. If one tired of community life, it was a simple matter to find solitude; the area in which they camped often bordered on true wilderness untouched by white men.

The delicately-posed child seen in the view at left is Grace Bloemer, daughter of the owner of the *Union Laundry Company* (see page 97). Scenic views such as this are uncommon and differ widely from Ericson's rigid studio portraits. Viewers of the scene might imagine that the young girl had paused for a moment in her bedroom window, but such a situation is most unlikely because of the photographer's slow films, bulky equipment, and the rather long preparation time leading to the production of an image. Despite these factors, the picture retains a gentle, candid quality.

The coronet band of Arcata play-
ed at the July Fourth celebration
of 1898. This picture was taken
on the town plaza, and Ericson's
brother Richard appears as the
third person from left. A. W.
Ericson's son Edgar may also be
seen, peering over the gentleman
to the left of the American flag
and over the heads of two of his
playmates.

On April 10, 1906, at the age of 58, A. W. Ericson travelled overland from Arcata to San Francisco where he had planned to relocate in the bustle of the big city. His wanderings placed him in downtown San Francisco on April 18, where he was engulfed in the catastrophic earthquake which destroyed much of the city. For several days the city burned, and Ericson wandered amidst the turmoil and confusion. Though most of his belongings had been destroyed in the collapse of the *Continental Hotel*, where he had been staying, he had retained a roll-film Autographic camera. He was thus able to take a number of pictures of the earthquake's aftermath, including this desolate view overlooking the Embarcadero area.

The parties of Dr. McKinnon (left) and Dr. Falk (right) provided a striking change to the appearance of Arcata when they paraded in their new automobiles shortly after the turn of the century. Dr. McKinnon was driving a curved dash 1903 Olds-mobile, while the car in which Dr. Falk is seated was probably a Dedion Bouton of about the same vintage. The steering apparatus on both machines were crude, though quite functional.

Catching the flavor, but not totally successful at stopping the motion of his subject, A. W. Ericson recorded the Golden Jubilee anniversary of Lodge Number 85, Independent Order of Odd Fellows on April 26, 1909. Because of the technical limitations of his film and lens, Ericson was unable to freeze the horse and whipping banners in the foreground. Even so, films were much improved over those which he had used 15 years earlier.

Arcata's plaza greatly resembles its contemporary appearance in this view taken about 1915. Residents of the city might notice that the now-towering palm trees planted on the square were not yet six feet tall, but the rows of parked automobiles provide a more striking visual clue to those not familiar with the town. From earliest times, the plaza served as a focus for Arcata's business and cultural events. Several of Ericson's business locations were situated on the plaza, and provided him with a window on the town's activities from 1877 to 1927.

The appearance of automobiles quickly changed in the early years. The Buick White Streak of 1908, with its powerful four cylinder motor and sleek lines undoubtedly provided its owner both with a sense of pride and a sore arm from cranking its engine. Within a few years after the introduction of the first automobiles, hundreds were purchased by citizens intrigued with the new machines. Although horses and wagons remained a part of the scene until nearly 1930, their role was fading notably by the time that this view was taken circa 1910.

In 1913, Henry Ford captured the country by storm with his one-color, four cylinder, Model T motorcar. Offering the rider such amenities as a windscreen, folding top, wide running boards, and soft leather upholstery, the cars were soon abundant throughout America. No Sunday was complete without a "drive around town," in which the riders sought to be seen as much as to see.

With the arrival of modern transportation, outlying areas quickly grew to importance. McKinleyville, located 10 miles north of Arcata, began as a cluster of buildings at roadside. Included was the *L. D. Graeter General Merchandise Store*. Graeter captured his share of passersby, with a wide range of food stuffs, vegetables, and automobile repair parts.

The car, because of its mechanical complexity, drew the blacksmith into the automobile repair field, and "service stations" grew overnight. The pork-pie hatted gentleman shown above was P. C. Sacchi, and was the proud proprietor of an auto repair service. As may be seen from the notices posted behind him on the wall, a customer was invited to buy and enjoy an "OK" used car, as long as he paid for it with "strictly cash."

Left to right, most members of the A. W. Ericson family may be seen in this view taken north of Arcata at Moonstone Beach: Edgar, Elsa, Mrs. Ella Ericson, Maude, Elma, Ella, Bruce MacMillan, Alice, and William. A. W. Ericson was, as usual, to be found behind the camera, but his familiar script signature which appeared on the reverse of most of his scenic views, may be found in the sand at his family's feet in the foreground.

Plate Credits

Pg. 88, William Balke; Pgs. 1, 2, 6, 11, 12, 13, 20, 44, 101, 102, 103, Dr. Robert V. Bryan; Pgs. 37, 72, Mrs. John E. Burman; Pg 81, Crescent City Public Library; Pgs. 31, 94, Asta Cullberg; Pgs 71, 76, 78, 97, 99, 100, Fountain Collection, Humboldt State University; Pgs. 67, 96, James G. Lundberg; Pgs. 10, 19, 21, 22, 24, 26, 28, 30, 32, 34, 35, 40, 41, 43, 45, 48, 49, 50, 51, 52, 54, 56, 57, 58, 59, 60, 61, 62, 63, 64, 65, 66, 68, 69, 70, 73, 75, 77, 79, 80, 82, 83, 84, 85, 86, 87, 89, 90, 91, 92, 93, 95, 98, 105, 106, 107, 108, 109, 110, Humboldt County Collection, Humboldt State University; Pgs. 27, 29, 33, 36, 38, 39, 46, 47, 53, 74, Humboldt County Historical Society; Pgs. 23, 42, 55, 104, Peter E. Palmquist; Pg. 8, Jere A. Smith; Pg 4, Gwyneth Susan; Pg. 25, Lillian O. Williams.